HOW TO DRAW
CARS and TRUCKS
and Other Vehicles

Barbara Soloff Levy

DOVER PUBLICATIONS, INC.
Mineola, New York

Bibliographical Note

How to Draw Cars and Trucks and Other Vehicles, first published in 2008, is a slightly altered republication of the edition published by Dover Publications, Inc., in 1994. "Practice Pages" have been added for this edition.

International Standard Book Number

ISBN-13: 978-0-486-46965-2
ISBN-10: 0-486-46965-4

Manufactured in the United States by LSC Communications
46965408   2017
www.doverpublications.com

Note

Cars and trucks—and bicycles, trains, and planes—are easy to draw. Look at them carefully and you will see that most of them are made up of very simple shapes, such as rectangles, triangles, and circles. All you have to do is draw the shapes and add details like windows and doors. This book has step-by-step diagrams for 28 different vehicles, from a sled to a fire engine—and everything in between!

To draw them, just follow the diagrams. Some erasing is called for, so be sure to use a pencil, not a pen. To get you started, let's draw the station wagon on page 2. First, draw a large rectangle with a smaller rectangle at one end, as shown in the top diagram. Draw a slanted line across each top corner of the large rectangle to shape the windshields, and across the front top corner of the smaller rectangle to form the hood. Erase the corners as shown by the broken lines. Next add circles for the wheels, erasing the straight lines inside them, and add a vertical line to form the door. Last, add the windows, hubcaps, and door handle. Opposite each drawing instruction page you will see a Practice Page, where you can practice your lines until you are ready to draw.

All of the vehicles are drawn in the same manner and are just as easy, so have a great time drawing your favorites!

HOW TO DRAW
CARS and TRUCKS
and Other Vehicles

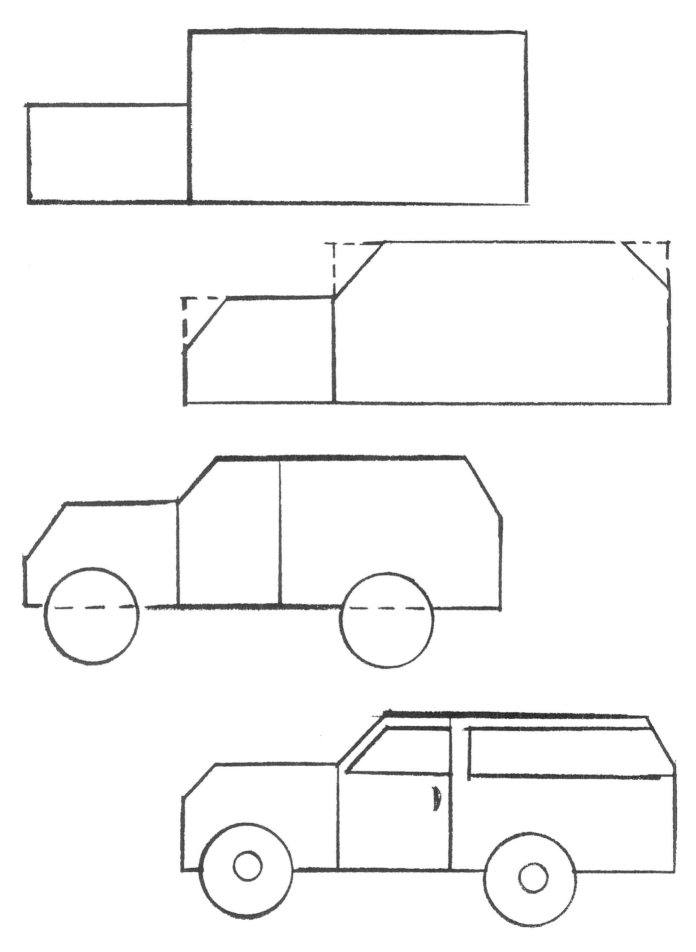

2 STATION WAGON

Practice Page

4   CAR (Side view)

Practice Page

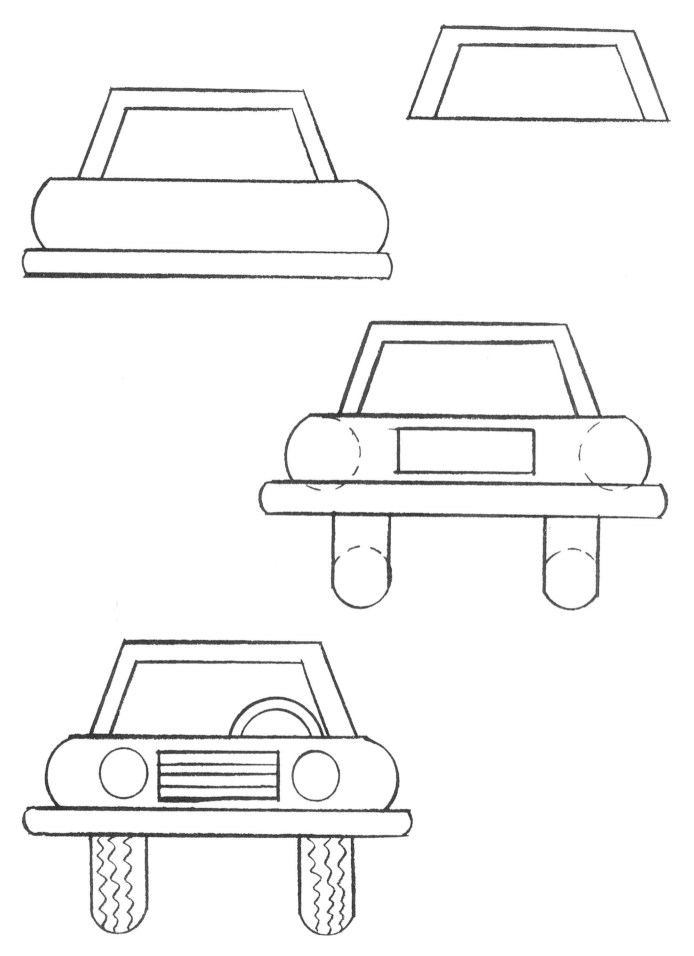

6   CAR (Front view)

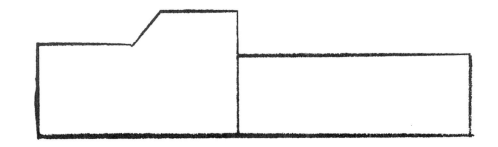

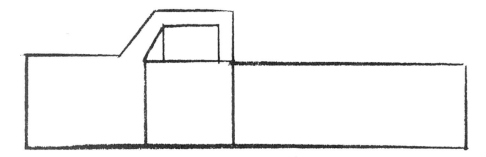

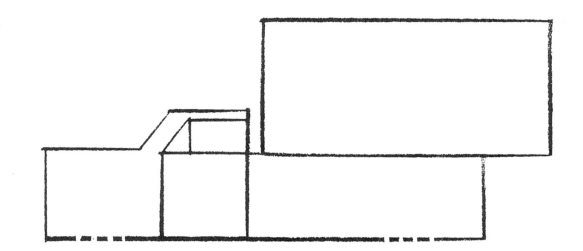

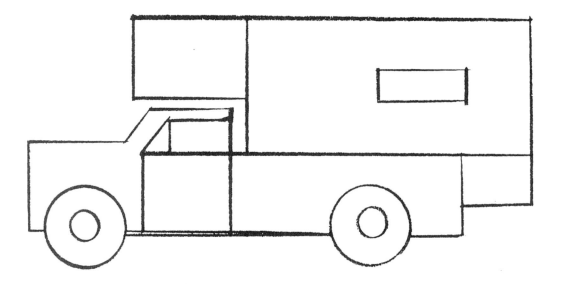

8   CAMPER

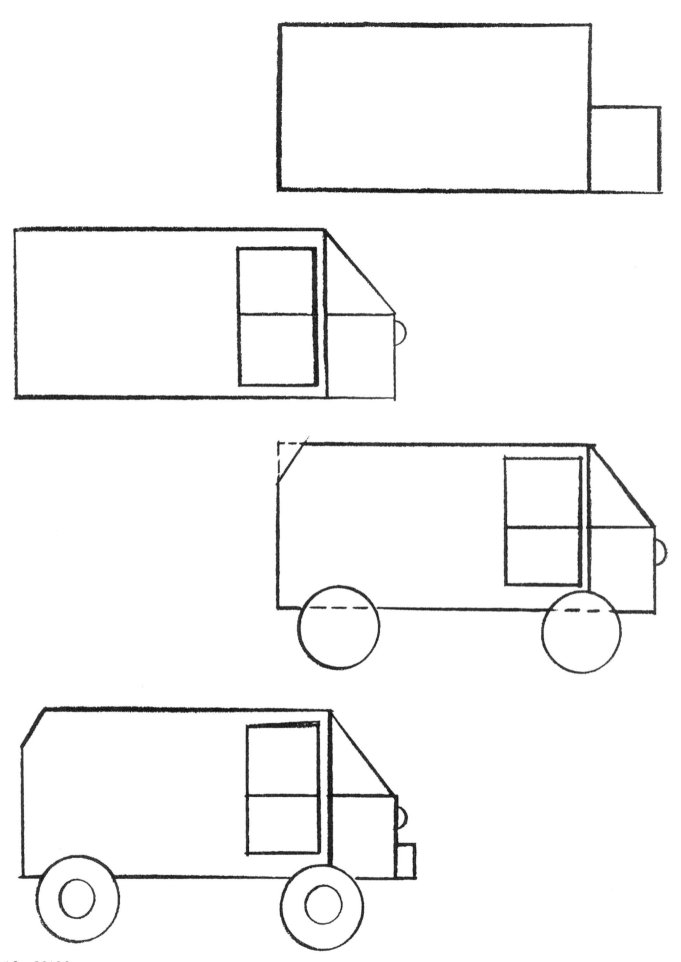

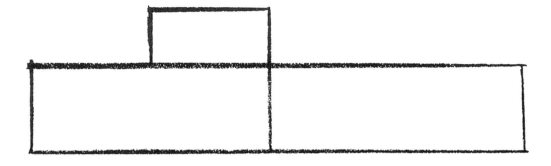

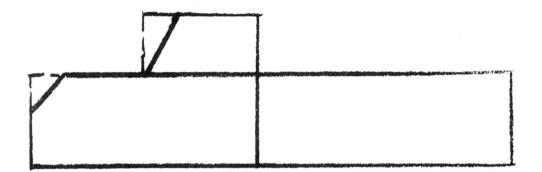

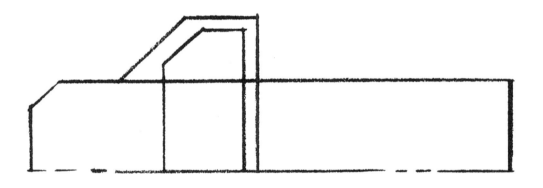

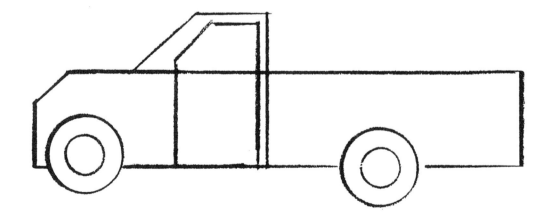

12   PICKUP TRUCK

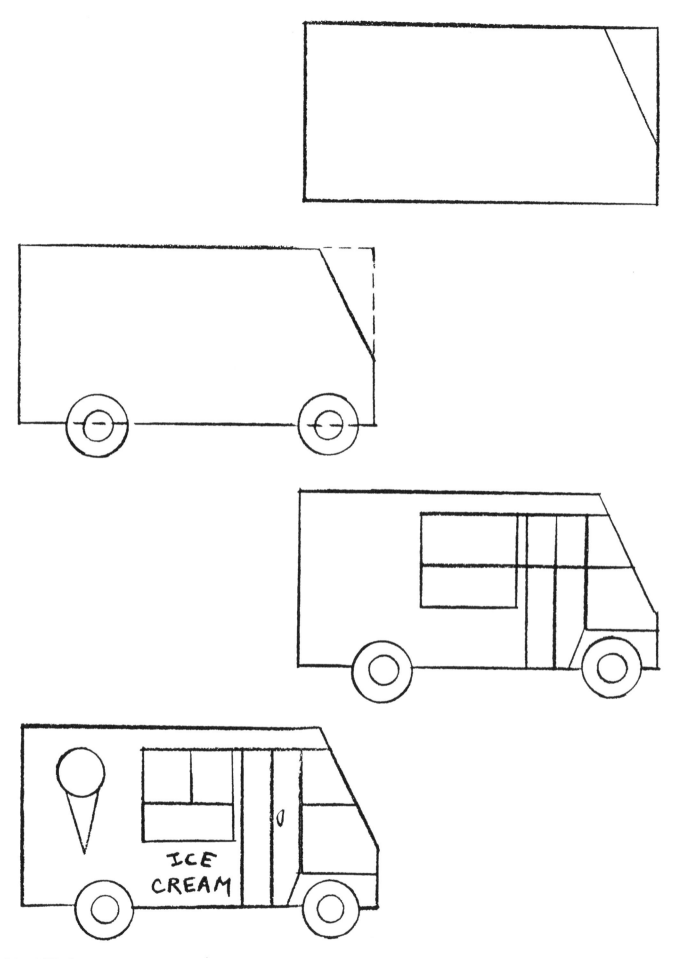

14   ICE CREAM TRUCK

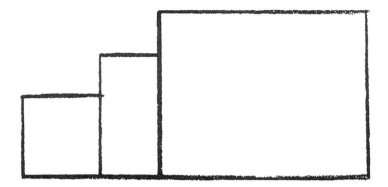

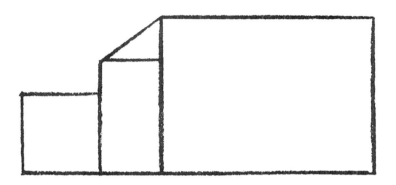

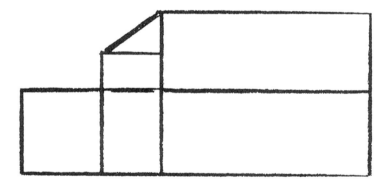

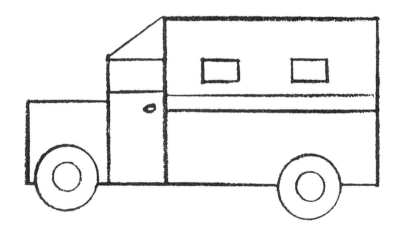

16   ARMORED TRUCK

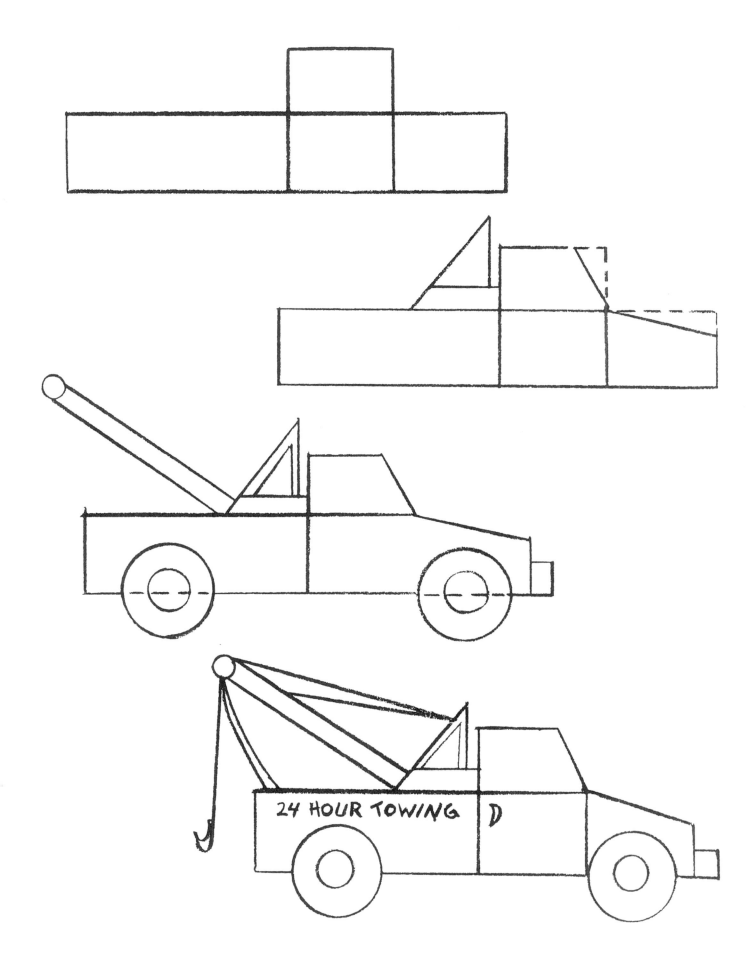

24 HOUR TOWING

D

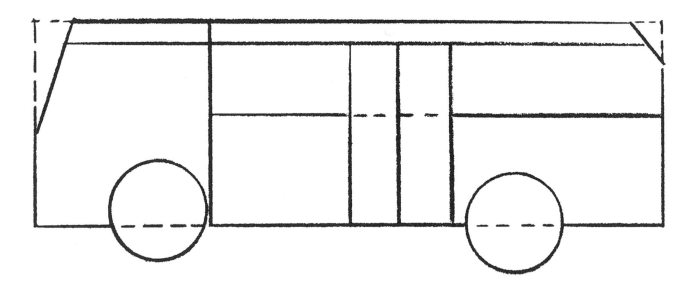

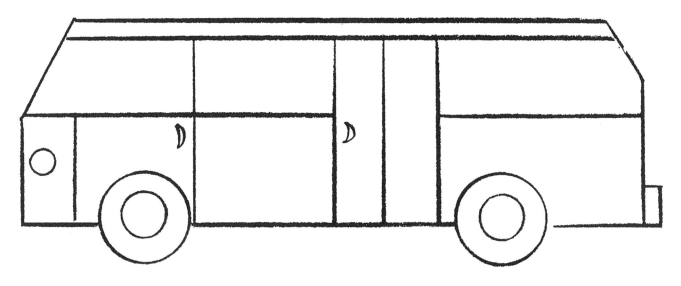

20   BUS

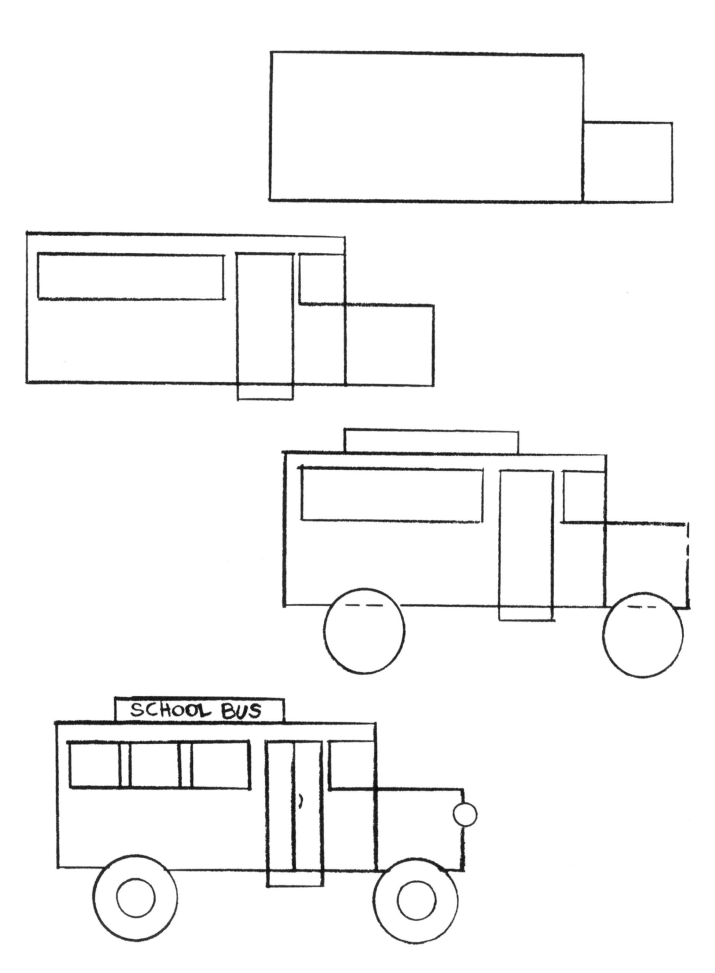

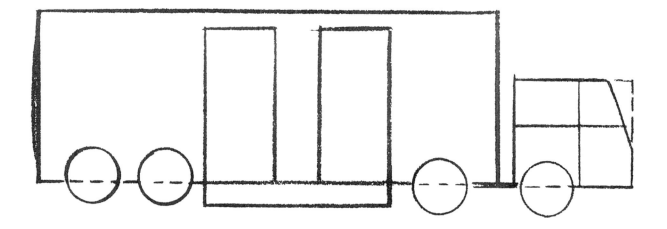

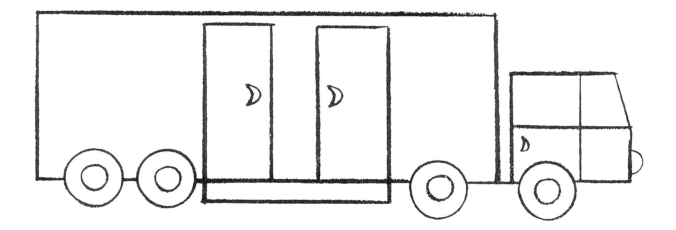

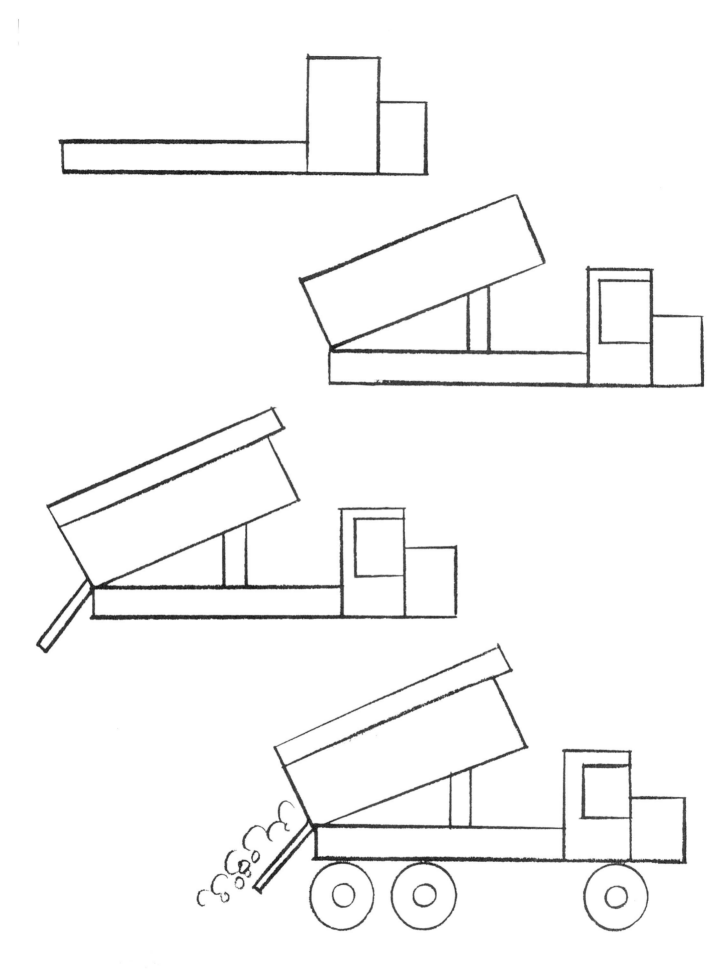

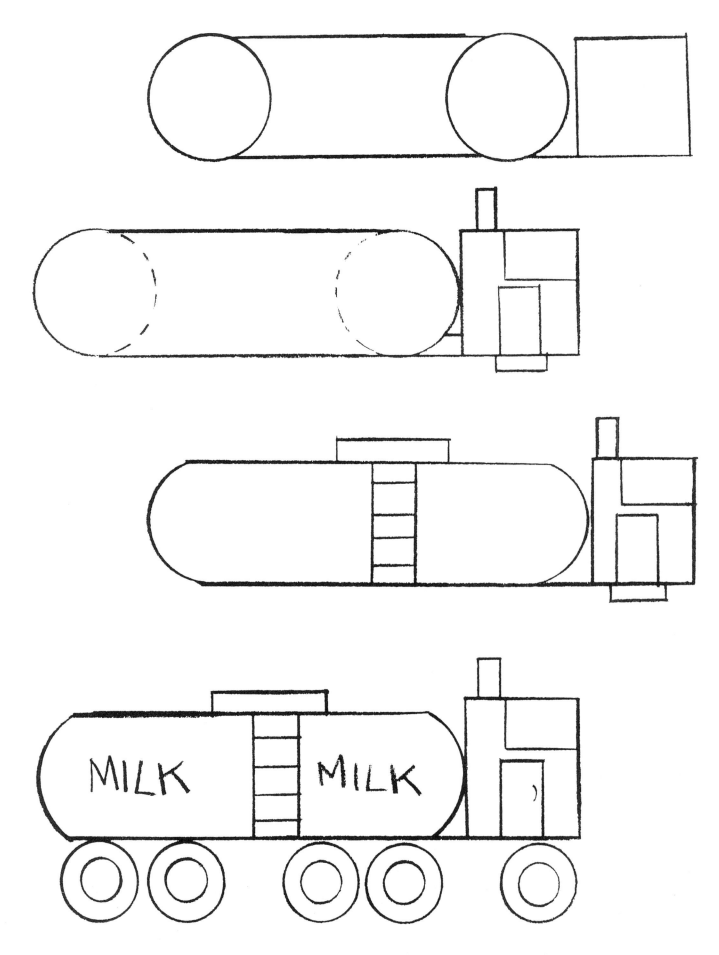

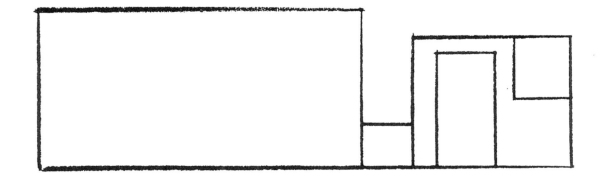

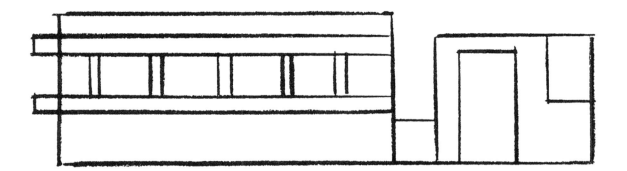

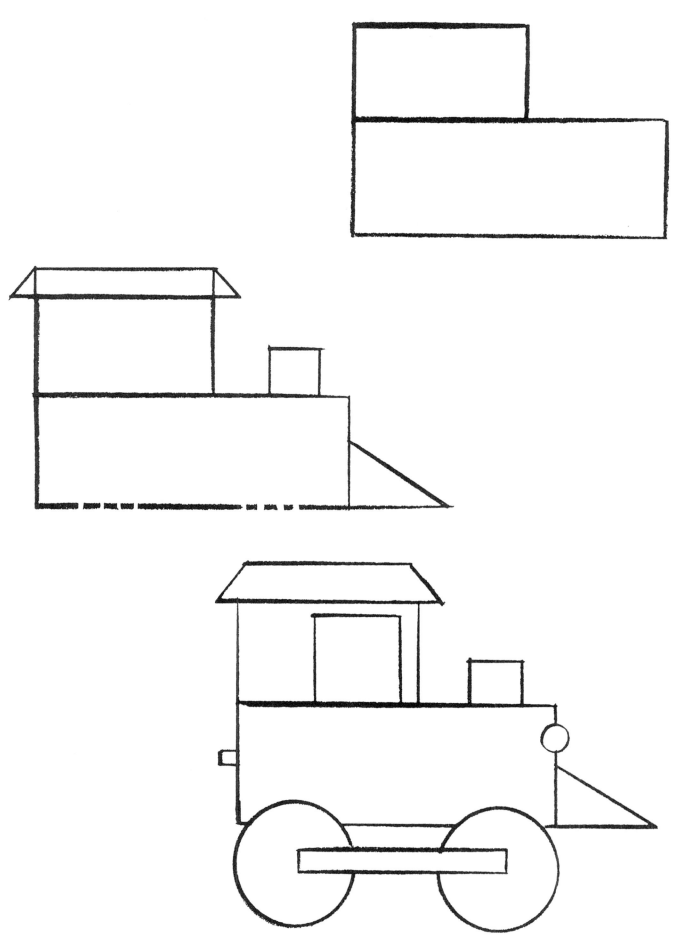

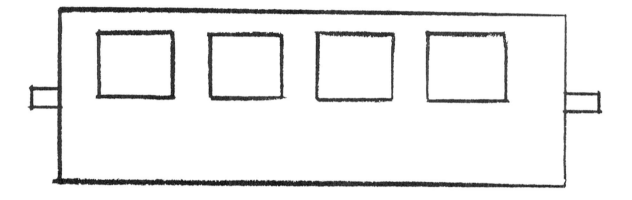

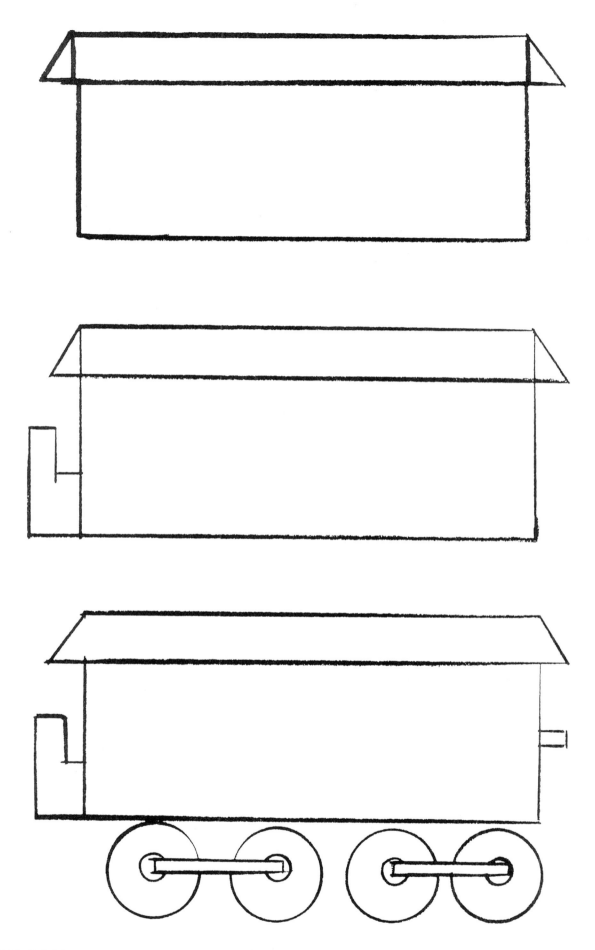

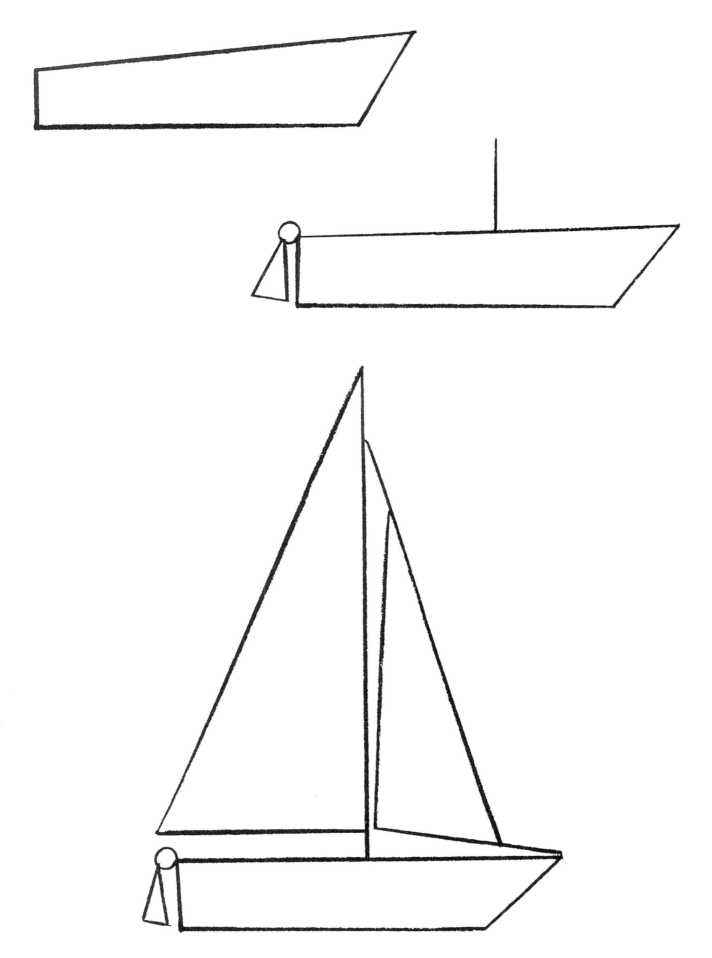

38 SAILBOAT

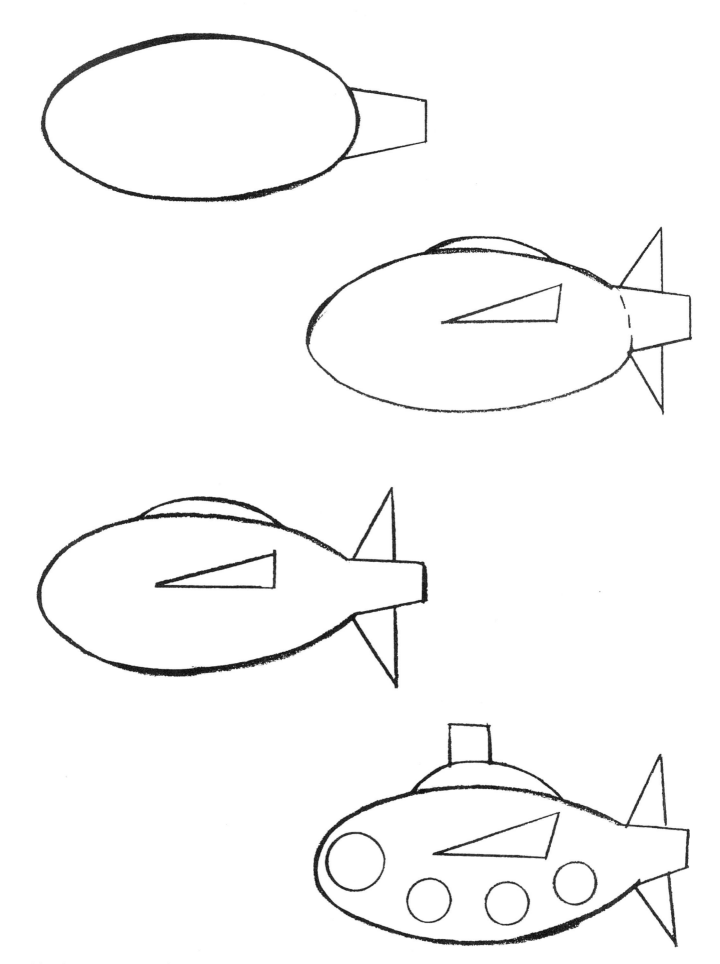

Practice Page

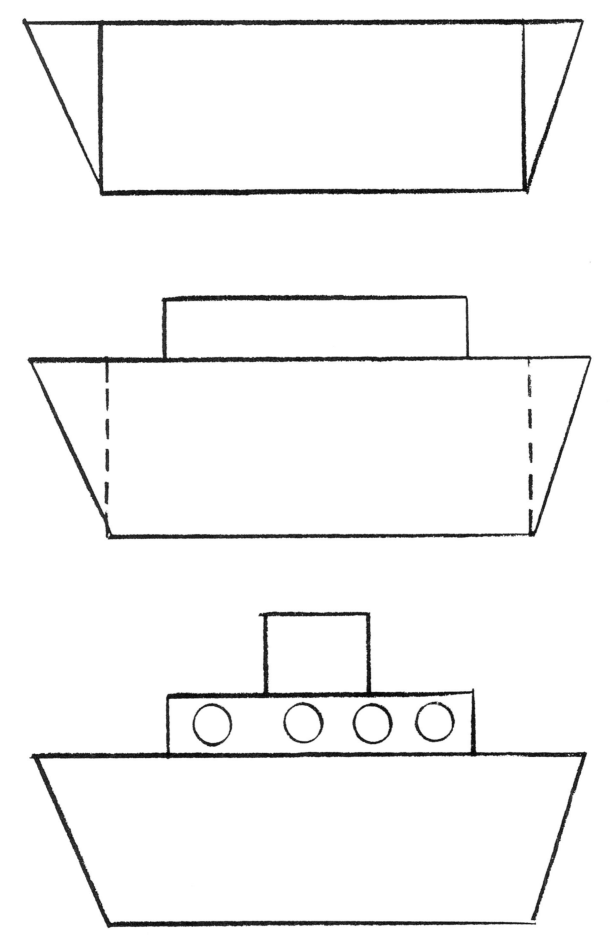

Practice Page

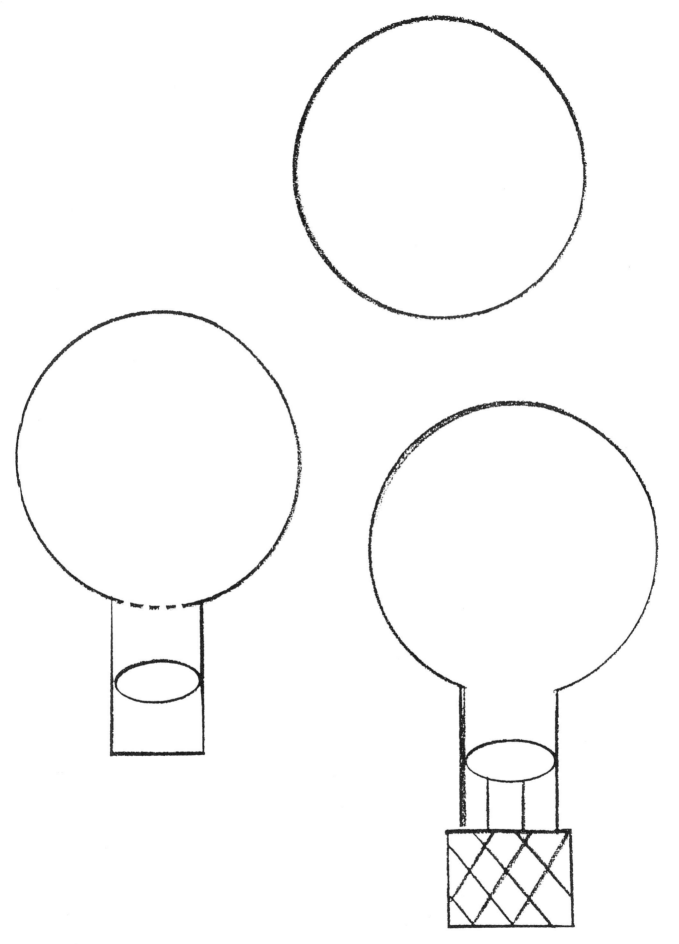

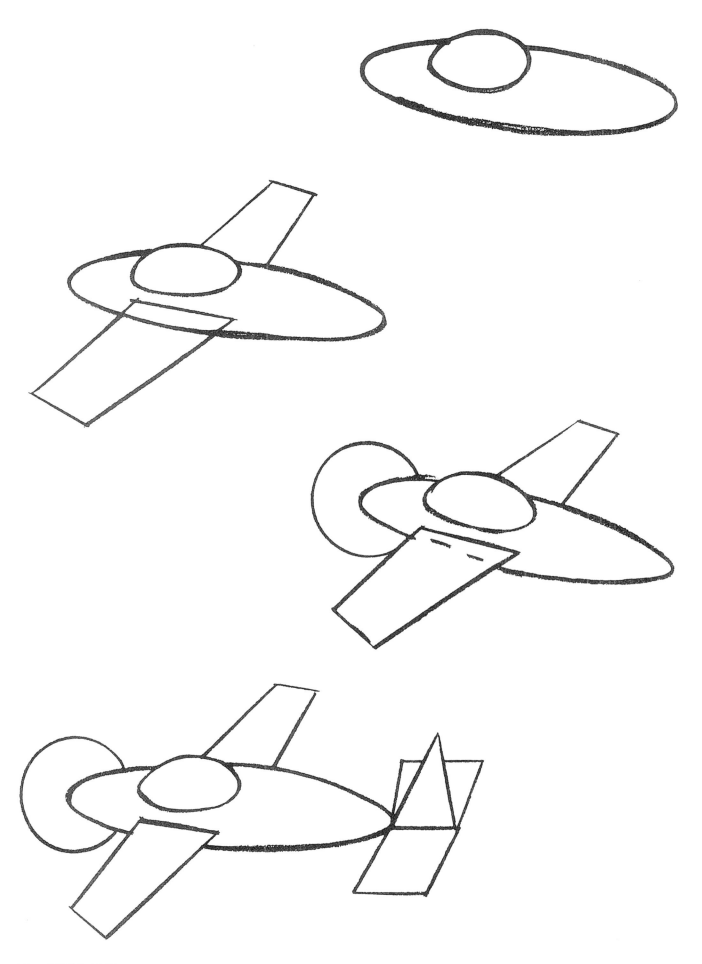

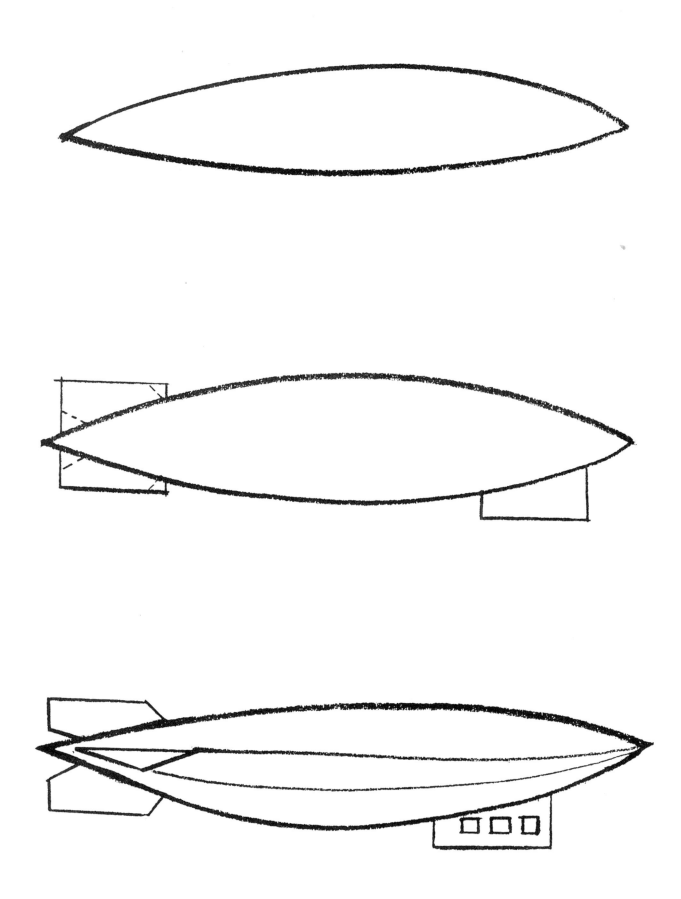

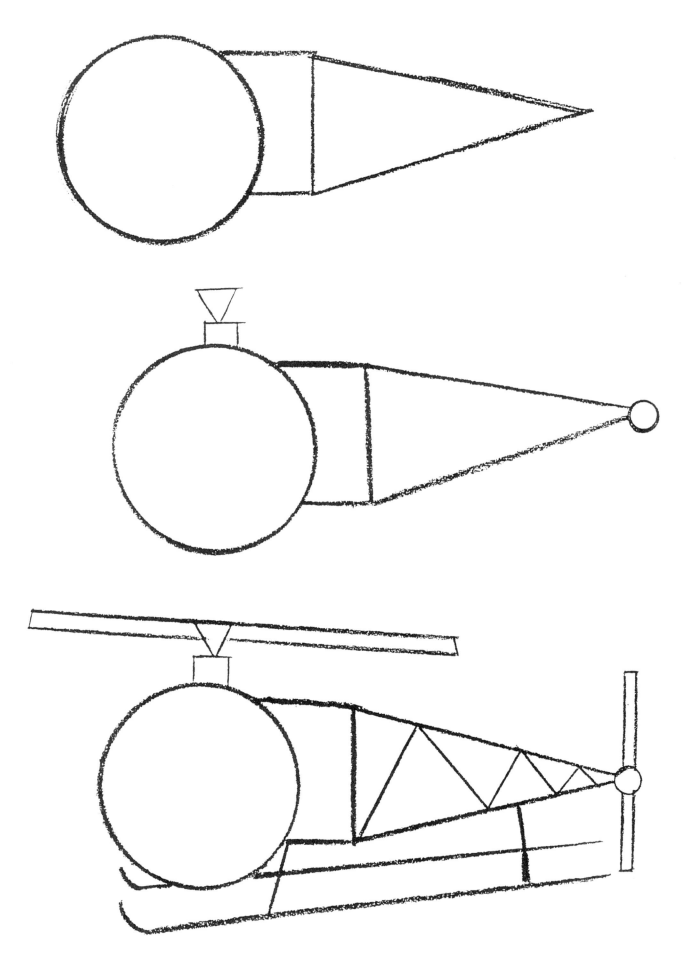

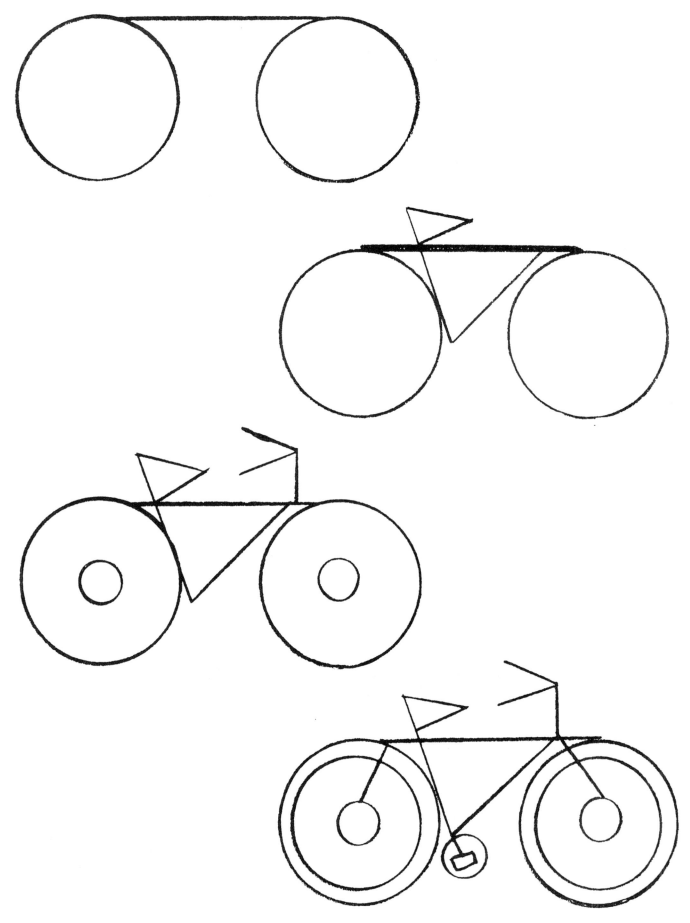

Practice Page

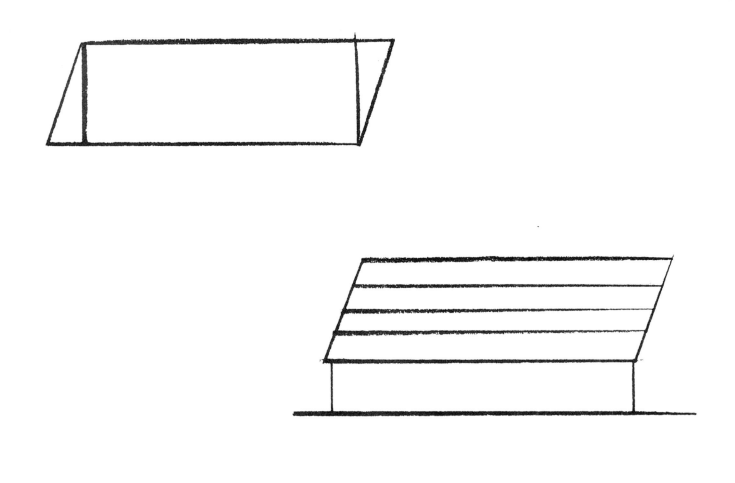

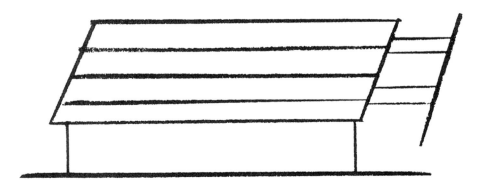

56   SLED